BECOMING A BIG BROTHER OR SISTER

A NEW BABY BOOK FOR SIBLINGS

Written by Darlene Stango, RNC

Illustrated by Rose Holtermann

Illustrations by Rose Holtermann
Layout and design by Julie Hodgins (www.juliekaren.com)

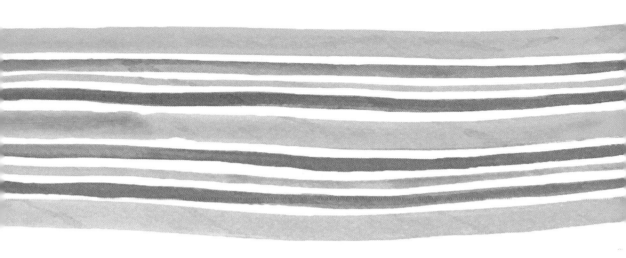

To my two sons,
CHRISTOPHER AND MATTHEW

There is so much
excitement at your
house. Mommy is bringing
home a new baby!

Did you know that the baby can see,
hear, smell, touch, taste, and make cooing
sounds? It is hard to believe that a baby
so small can do all of these things.

The bones in the baby's head are soft and open in some spots. That is one of the reasons that everyone holds the baby very carefully. Mommy will have you wash your hands and sit down before you hold the baby. An adult will help you by holding the baby's head and neck.

You can help mommy by helping her
get all of the things ready that the
baby needs to take a bath. Once
mommy starts giving the baby
a bath, she can't leave the baby
alone, not even for a second!

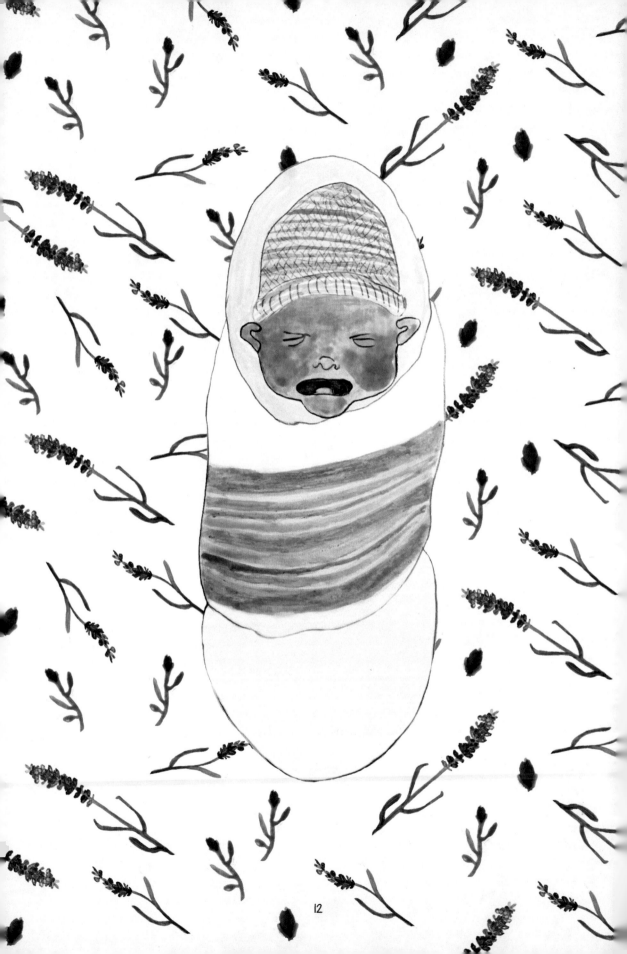

Some new babies cry a lot. Crying is the baby's way of saying that it needs something. Mommy will try to figure out what that is. The baby is trying to let us know that it is hungry, or tired, or warm, or cold, or that it needs its diaper changed.

New babies need their diapers changed
around eight times a day. A clean, dry
diaper keeps the baby comfortable
and without a rash on its bottom.

The baby may be trying
to tell mommy that it is
hungry when it cries.

Babies grow quickly, so
they need to eat as often
as every few hours.

Sometimes, no one can figure out what the baby needs when it is crying, not even mommy. When that happens, mommy will just have to put the baby down in the crib, walk away, and let the baby cry. Hopefully, the baby is just tired and will soon fall asleep.

As the baby gets older and starts
to crawl, it will be interested in your
toys and books. Keep them in a safe
place. Adults can read your books
to both of you. It doesn't matter
that the baby doesn't understand
them like you do. What matters to
the baby is that he or she is being
talked to and smiled at and held
close. Spending time together is how
you will get to know each other.

24

You will be having a lot of different
moods and feelings now that the
new baby is here, good feelings as
well as not-so-good feelings. This is
how big brothers and sisters feel.
Remember that mommy and daddy
love you just as much as they ever did.
The not-so-good feelings will pass.

There is only one you in the whole wide world, who mommy and daddy once took care of, just like they are taking care of the new baby. You are even MORE special now than you ever were.

YOU ARE A BIG SISTER OR BROTHER!

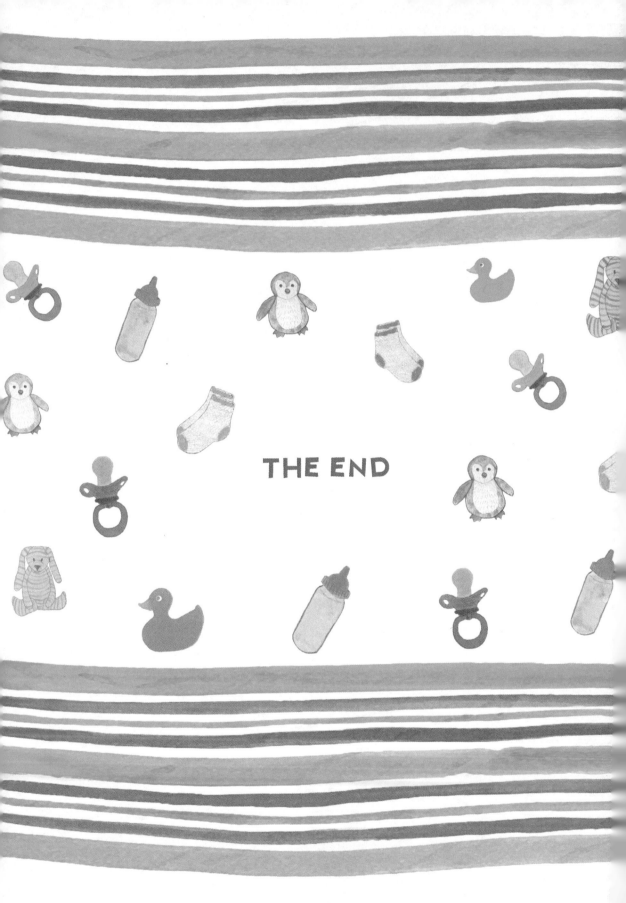

THE END

Made in the USA
Las Vegas, NV
23 January 2023

66138247R00019